THE NEW AMERICAN DICTIONARY

INTERACTIVE SECURITY★FEAR EDITION

Compiled by the Institute for Infinitely Small Things

Published by the Institute for Infinitely Small Things, 144 Moody Street, Bldg 4, Waltham, MA, 02453, USA. info@infinitelysmallthings.net.

This special paperback edition produced in association with and exclusively for the Institute for Infinitely Small Things.

Terms compiled via research conducted at PURE, an experiment in Allston, MA, curated by Lisa Gordon in Fall 2006.

The right to define certain terms that appear in this publication was sold to contributers via eBay.com for various amounts of money during a week-long auction that ended 12/25/2006 in accordance with the rules laid out by ebayaday, an exhibition curated by Rebekah Modrak, Aaron Ahuvia and Zackery Denfeld.

Definitions authored by the auction-winners as follows:
Robert Arnold, Shannon Coyle, Robert Ek, John Krygier, Carrie Lambert-Beatty, Savić Rašović, Owen Smith, Phil Taylor.

This project is made possible by iKatun, a non-profit organization dedicated to presenting contemporary art that fosters public engagement in the politics of information.

Printed in the United States.

The Institute for Infinitely Small Things
www.infinitelysmallthings.net

ISBN 978-1-4303-1986-3

TABLE OF CONTENTS

★ bolded entries denote definitions supplied by eBay auction winners

FREE
By purchasing this dictionary, you own the right to define this term free of charge.

ACTIONABLE

(āk'shə-nə-bəl) adj.

Write your definition in the space below.

FREE
By purchasing this dictionary, you own the right to define this term free of charge.

ACT OF WAR

(ākt-ŭv-wôr) n.

Write your definition in the space below.

FREE
By purchasing this dictionary, you own the right to define this term free of charge.

ALERT

(ə-lûrt') n.

Write your definition in the space below.

FREE
By purchasing this dictionary, you own the right to define this term free of charge.

ASYMMETRIC WARFARE

(ā'sĭ-mĕt'rĭk wôr'fâr') n.

Write your definition in the space below.

$7.16
Robert Ek of Malmö,
Sweden, purchased
the right to define
this term on eBay on
12/25/06.

AXIS OF EVIL

(āk'sĭs-ŭv-ē'vəl) n.

(1) A dialectical figure creating meaning to assist the proprietor's desire to isolate the question at issue, generally geo-political, by encircling dissolute gatherings from their lowest common denominator - namely their deviance from the proprietors agenda - who in his turn substantiates affiliation primarily by the dialectical figures characteristic as contradictory.

(2) Also applicable in everyday situations for meter maids, journalists and umpires.

Definition courtesy of bekant.org (Robert Ek & Niklas Qvarnström).

FREE
By purchasing this dictionary, you own the right to define this term free of charge.

BIOTERRORISM

(bī'ō-těr'ə-rĭz'əm) n.

Write your definition in the space below.

FREE
By purchasing this dictionary, you own the right to define this term free of charge.

BLACK SITE

(blāk-sīt) n.

Write your definition in the space below.

FREE
By purchasing this dictionary, you own the right to define this term free of charge.

BOMBING CAMPAIGN

(bŏm-ēn-kām-pān') n.

Write your definition in the space below.

$12.84
Phil Taylor of Seattle, WA, purchased the right to define this term on eBay on 12/25/06*.

COALITION OF THE WILLING

(kō'ə-lĭsh'ən-ŭv-thə-wĭl'ĭng) n.

49 States who have at least one soldier on the ground in Iraq or are publicly committed to the Coalition. The countries are:

Afghanistan	Marshall Islands
Albania	Micronesia
Angola	Mongolia
Australia	Netherlands
Azerbaijan	Nicaragua
Bulgaria	Palau
Colombia	Panama
Czech Republic	Philippines
Denmark	Poland
Dominican Republic	Portugal
El Salvador	Romania
Eritrea	Rwanda
Estonia	Singapore
Ethiopia	Slovakia
Georgia	Solomon Islands
Honduras	South Korea
Hungary	Spain
Iceland	Tonga
Italy	Turkey
Japan	Uganda
Kuwait	Ukraine
Latvia	United Kingdom
Lithuania	United States
Macedonia	Uzbekistan

* - Right to define "Coalition of the Willing" gifted by Phil Taylor to Shannon Coyle of Cambridge, MA, on 01/24/07.

FREE
By purchasing this dictionary, you own the right to define this term free of charge.

CONFLICT

(kŏn'flĭkt') n.

Write your definition in the space below.

FREE
By purchasing this dictionary, you own the right to define this term free of charge.

CONFLICT RESOLUTION

(kŏn'flĭkt' rĕz'ə-lōō'shən) n.

Write your definition in the space below.

FREE
By purchasing this dictionary, you own the right to define this term free of charge.

CUT AND RUN

(kŭt-ən-rŭn) v.

Write your definition in the space below.

FREE
By purchasing this dictionary, you own the right to define this term free of charge.

DECIDER

(dĭ-sī'-dər) n.

Write your definition in the space below.

FREE
By purchasing this dictionary, you own the right to define this term free of charge.

DEMOCRACY

(dĭ-mŏk'rə-sē) n.

Write your definition in the space below.

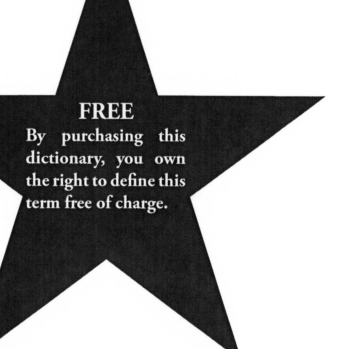

FREE
By purchasing this dictionary, you own the right to define this term free of charge.

DUCT TAPE

(dŭk-tāp) n.

Write your definition in the space below.

$15.50
Carrie Lambert-Beatty
of Cambridge, MA,
purchased the right
to define this term on
eBay on 12/25/06.

EMBEDDED JOURNALIST

(ĕm-bĕd'-ĕd-jûr'nə-lĭst) n.

(1) An innovation in media-military relations developed by the Pentagon and Department of Defense during the second US-Iraq war. From journalist (a person who practices the profession of journalism) and embedded (enclosed completely in a surrounding mass).

(2) A military tool for information management. Instead of allowing journalists freedom of movement and access and risking negative reporting from the front (see: Vietnam War), contracts greater safety and access for journalists to up-close stories about the life of a U.S. military unit, in exchange for limits on their reporting.

(3) A media tool for ratings management. In-depth, research-driven, carefully produced stories providing historical perspective and multiple points of view on the war are replaced by the immediacy of live if grainy videophone images and the human-interest potential of a reporter's personal involvement with a single military battalion or unit.

(4) A reporter doing her best to tell the stories of military units at war, despite the best efforts of media and military powers to tame, restrict, and edit her.

FREE
By purchasing this dictionary, you own the right to define this term free of charge.

ENEMY

(ĕn'ə-mē) n.

Write your definition in the space below.

FREE
By purchasing this dictionary, you own the right to define this term free of charge.

ENEMY COMBATANT

(ĕn'ə-mē-kəm-bāt'nt) n.

Write your definition in the space below.

FREE
By purchasing this dictionary, you own the right to define this term free of charge.

EXECUTIVE POWERS

(ĭg-zĕk'yə-tĭv-pou'ərz) n.

Write your definition in the space below.

FREE
By purchasing this dictionary, you own the right to define this term free of charge.

EVILDOERS

(ē'vəl-dōō'ərs) n.

Write your definition in the space below.

$10.49
Owen Smith of Bangor, Maine, purchased the right to define this term on eBay on 12/25/06.

EXIT STRATEGY

(ĕk'sĭt-strāt'ə-jē) n.

(1)

(2)

(3)

(4)

(5)

(6)

See also Strategery - http://www.reference.com/browse/wiki/Strategery.

FREE
By purchasing this dictionary, you own the right to define this term free of charge.

EXTRAORDINARY RENDITION

(ĭk-strôr'dn-ĕr'ē-rĕn-dĭsh'ən) n.

Write your definition in the space below.

FREE
By purchasing this dictionary, you own the right to define this term free of charge.

FREEDOM

(frē'dəm) n.

Write your definition in the space below.

FREE
By purchasing this
dictionary, you own
the right to define this
term free of charge.

FREEDOM FRIES

(frē'dəm-frīz) n.

Write your definition in the space below.

FREE
By purchasing this dictionary, you own the right to define this term free of charge.

FREEDOM-HATING

(frē'dəm-hāt-ĭng) adj.

Write your definition in the space below.

FREE
By purchasing this dictionary, you own the right to define this term free of charge.

FREEDOM-LOVING

(frē′dəm-lŭv-ĭng) adj.

Write your definition in the space below.

$0.01
Savić   Rašović   of
Cambridge, MA, pur-
chased the right to de-
fine this term on eBay
on 12/25/06.

FRIENDLY FIRE

(frĕnd'lē-fīr) n.

(1) An ancient custom of storytelling around a campfire.

(2) An intense relationship, a.k.a "fuck friends".

(3) A Burning Man event involving large amounts of dangerous but friendly fire installations.

(4) Blue on blue. Originally from British English indicating a mistaken exchange between teammates.

(5) An online multiplayer server game setting: Friendly Fire ON/OFF. Also referred to as FF ON/OFF.

(6) A public and temporary PR battle between friends, a.k.a Paris Hilton vs. Nicole Ritchie.

(7) A musical, surreal fantasy on the themes of love and friendship, set to the music and songs of the Sean Lennon album "Friendly Fire".

FREE
By purchasing this dictionary, you own the right to define this term free of charge.

FUNDAMENTALISTS

(fŭn'də-měn'tl-ĭzts) n.

Write your definition in the space below.

FREE
By purchasing this dictionary, you own the right to define this term free of charge.

GENDER POLICING

(jĕn'dər-pə-lēs'-ĭng) tr.v.

Write your definition in the space below.

FREE
By purchasing this dictionary, you own the right to define this term free of charge.

GOD

(gŏd) n.

Write your definition in the space below.

FREE
By purchasing this dictionary, you own the right to define this term free of charge.

GROUND ZERO

(ground-zē'rō) n.

Write your definition in the space below.

FREE
By purchasing this
dictionary, you own
the right to define this
term free of charge.

ILLEGAL ALIEN

(ĭ-lē′gəl-ā′lē-ən) n.

Write your definition in the space below.

FREE
By purchasing this dictionary, you own the right to define this term free of charge.

IMMINENT THREAT

(ĭm'ə-nənt-thrĕt) n.

Write your definition in the space below.

FREE
By purchasing this dictionary, you own the right to define this term free of charge.

INSURGENCY

(ĭn-sûr′jən-sē) n.

Write your definition in the space below.

FREE
By purchasing this dictionary, you own the right to define this term free of charge.

ISLAMOFASCIST

(ĭs'läm'ō-fāsh'ĭst) n.

Write your definition in the space below.

FREE
By purchasing this dictionary, you own the right to define this term free of charge.

JUSTICE

(jŭs'tĭs) n.

Write your definition in the space below.

FREE
By purchasing this dictionary, you own the right to define this term free of charge.

MASS DESTRUCTION

(mās-dĭ-strŭk'shən) n.

Write your definition in the space below.

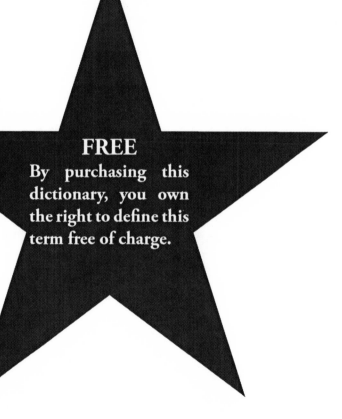

FREE
By purchasing this
dictionary, you own
the right to define this
term free of charge.

OUR WAY OF LIFE

(our-wā-ŭv-līf) n.

Write your definition in the space below.

FREE
By purchasing this dictionary, you own the right to define this term free of charge.

PATRIOT ACT

(pā′trē-ət-ākt) n.

Write your definition in the space below.

FREE
By purchasing this dictionary, you own the right to define this term free of charge.

PATRIOTIC

(pā'trē-ət'ĭk) adj.

Write your definition in the space below.

$6.27
Owen Smith of Bangor, ME, purchased the right to define this term on eBay on 12/25/06.

PREEMPTIVE WAR

(prē-ĕmp'tĭv-wôr) n.

(1) Of, relating to, or characteristic of a politically motivated action, often used to deflect attention from other more pressing concerns.

(2) A political "sleight of hand" used to distract or delude an unaware or uneducated populace in which a perceived threat is acted upon with little or no demonstrable basis in fact or reality.

(3) Apocalyptic rhetoric used to justify a violation of international law or treaties.

(4) Having or marked by the power to preempt or take precedence through an act of war, what is called alternatively "forward deterrence" or "anticipatory self-defense," but in all cases an act that is generally considered to fall short of the requirements of a just war.

FREE
By purchasing this dictionary, you own the right to define this term free of charge.

PREPAREDNESS

(prĭ-pâr'ĭd-nĭs) n.

Write your definition in the space below.

FREE
By purchasing this dictionary, you own the right to define this term free of charge.

RACIAL PROFILING

(rā'shəl-prō'fīl'ĭng) tr.v.

Write your definition in the space below.

FREE
By purchasing this dictionary, you own the right to define this term free of charge.

RADICAL IDEOLOGY

(rād'ĭ-kəl-ī'dē-ŏl'ə-jē) n.

Write your definition in the space below.

FREE
By purchasing this dictionary, you own the right to define this term free of charge.

READINESS

(rĕd'ē-nĭs) n.

Write your definition in the space below.

REGIME CHANGE

(rā-zhēm' chānj) n.

Write your definition in the space below.

FREE
By purchasing this dictionary, you own the right to define this term free of charge.

REIGN OF TERROR

(rān-ŭv-tĕr'ər) n.

Write your definition in the space below.

FREE
By purchasing this dictionary, you own the right to define this term free of charge.

SECTARIAN VIOLENCE

(sĕk-târ'ē-ən-vī'ə-ləns) n.

Write your definition in the space below.

FREE
By purchasing this dictionary, you own the right to define this term free of charge.

SECURITY

(sĭ-kyoor'ĭ-tē) n.

Write your definition in the space below.

FREE
By purchasing this dictionary, you own the right to define this term free of charge.

SHOCK AND AWE

(shŏk-ənd-ô) n., adj., & v.

Write your definition in the space below.

FREE
By purchasing this
dictionary, you own
the right to define this
term free of charge.

SLEEPER CELL

(slē′pər-sĕl) n.

Write your definition in the space below.

FREE
By purchasing this dictionary, you own the right to define this term free of charge.

SMART BOMB

(smärt-bŏm) n.

Write your definition in the space below.

FREE
By purchasing this dictionary, you own the right to define this term free of charge.

SURGE

(sûrj) n.

Write your definition in the space below.

FREE
By purchasing this dictionary, you own the right to define this term free of charge.

SURVEILLANCE

(sər-vā′ləns) n.

Write your definition in the space below.

$7.50
Robert Arnold of Qualicum Beach, BC, Canada, purchased the right to define this term on eBay on 12/25/06.

TERROR

(tĕr'ər) n.

(1) Extreme fear.

(2) An irrational fear of foreign enemies and potential threats, instilled in the public by a government, often in collusion with corporate interests, and promulgated by the media they control. The objective is to create a state of mind wherein people will be willing to relenquish their rights and freedom, and submit to a degree of government monitoring and control that would be unthinkable in a free society, in exchange for the government's hollow promise of protection.

(3) The stated goal of small, suicidally violent groups of political and/or religious fanatics who follow the rhetoric of madmen. Their occasional acts of violence ultimately benefit the governments against which the violence is directed by providing material for the media to feed on and justification for the government to increase the repression of its citizens.

(4) The fear that results from the realization that one has overextended one's credit to the point where any hope of repayment is futile, and that the rest of one's life will be an endless struggle for survival under an increasing burden of debt. This condition is promoted by banking and business interests to (a) insure that people will remain docile workers who, despite being overworked and underpaid, will do nothing to endanger the jobs that enable them to barely keep up with their debts, and (b) generate increasing profits by facilitating further debt and encouraging consumers to aspire to a carefully marketed lifestyle, so they will continue to spend that which they do not have for that which they do not need.

(5) The feeling that comes with the realization that we are all responsible for the conditions of our lives, and for permitting the preceding definitions to exist.

(6) A barrier to transcend on the road to freedom and enlightenment.

FREE
By purchasing this dictionary, you own the right to define this term free of charge.

TERRORIST

(tĕr'ər-ĭst) n.

Write your definition in the space below.

FREE
By purchasing this
dictionary, you own
the right to define this
term free of charge.

THEM

(thĕm) pron.

Write your definition in the space below.

FREE
By purchasing this dictionary, you own the right to define this term free of charge.

TIMETABLE

(tīm'tā'bəl) n.

Write your definition in the space below.

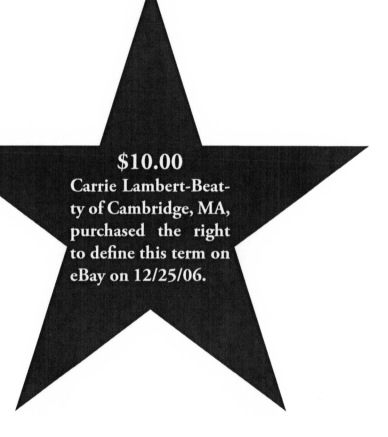

$10.00
Carrie Lambert-Beat-
ty of Cambridge, MA,
purchased the right
to define this term on
eBay on 12/25/06.

TORTURE

(tôr'chər) n.

(1) The infliction of extreme physical or psychological pain (obsolete).

(2) A shifting formulary of behaviors linguistically manipulated and defined by agents and agencies of power so as to allow extreme physical or psychological pain to be inflicted by those agents and agencies.

FREE
By purchasing this dictionary, you own the right to define this term free of charge.

TRANSFER OF TERRORISTS

(trāns'fər-ŭv-tĕr'ər-ĭsts) n.

Write your definition in the space below.

FREE
By purchasing this dictionary, you own the right to define this term free of charge.

UNILATERAL

(yōō'nə-lāt'ər-əl) adj.

Write your definition in the space below.

$6.94
John Krygier of Delaware, OH, purchased the right to define this term on eBay on 12/25/06.

UNMARKED PACKAGE

(ŭn-märkt'pāk'ĭj) n.

(1a) An object of unmitigated and consummate fear among the public, typically compact, portable, rectangular, and tannish in hue, used for crowd control, auditorium clearing, dispersal of protesters and others gathering in public spaces for unpatriotic reasons. Also used for Homeland Security drills.

(1b) An object of unmitigated and consummate desire among the public, typically compact, portable, rectangular, and tannish in hue, used for the delivery of Viagra, gay porn, penis enhancers, breast enhancers, birth control, vibrators, Brittany Spears cds, etc.

(1c) (obsolete) A box containing a gift or other pleasant item, delivered by the mailman.

(2a) A requirement of the U.S. Postal Service (regulation 65-577 A, part C2, section 2, paragraph 8, sub-paragraph 5.3, abit down on the page), instituted in early 2002, for any package delivered by the U.S. Postal Service: "If thou shall reuse a fabricated wood-product receptacle, and if thou shall observe uponst thust fabricated wood-product receptacle, uponst inspection, a badge, blaze, brand, character, device, distinction, earmark, emblem, evidence, feature, hallmark, idiosyncrasy, image, impression, incision, indication, indicia, label, marking, note, particularity, peculiarity, print, proof, property, seal, sign, significant, stamp, symbol, symptom, token, trait, or type, then thou shall de-badge, de-blaze, de-brand, de-character, de-device, de-distinction, de-earmark, de-emblem, de-evidence, de-feature, de-hallmark, de-idiosyncrasy, de-image, de-impression, de-incision, de-indication, de-indicia, de-label, de-mark, de-note, de-particular, de-peculiar, de-print, de-proof, de-property, de-seal, de-sign, de-significant, de-stamp, de-symbol, de-symptom, de-token, de-trait, or de-type said fabricated wood-product receptacle prior to relegating custody of said fabricated wood-product receptacle to the U.S. Postal Service."

(2b) The shock and awe generated among the fearful public by the postal worker, able to consort with and purvey the "unmarked package" with no apparent self harm (e.g., "I'unmarked packaged' that frumpy housewife.").

FREE
By purchasing this dictionary, you own the right to define this term free of charge.

US

(ŭs & yōō-ĕs') pron. & n.

Write your definition in the space below.

FREE
By purchasing this dictionary, you own the right to define this term free of charge.

VICTORY

(vĭk'tə-rē) n.

Write your definition in the space below.

FREE
By purchasing this dictionary, you own the right to define this term free of charge.

WAR ON TERROR

(wôr-ŏn-tĕr'ər) n.

Write your definition in the space below.

FREE
By purchasing this dictionary, you own the right to define this term free of charge.

WAR ROOM

(wôr-rōōm) n.

Write your definition in the space below.

FREE
By purchasing this dictionary, you own the right to define this term free of charge.

WATERBOARDING

(wô'tər-bôrd'ĭng) tr.v.

Write your definition in the space below.

FREE
By purchasing this dictionary, you own the right to define this term free of charge.

WITHDRAWAL

(wĭth-drô'əl) n.

Write your definition in the space below.

Should your definition/s be included in the next edition?

Want to suggest a new or recently re-defined Fear/Security term?

Send your definitions and suggestions to info@infinitelysmallthings.net

The Institute for Infinitely Small Things

www.infinitelysmallthings.net

The Institute for Infinitely Small Things uses performance in public space to research and alter the micro-power structures that shape everyday life in Western society. These social and political tiny things have included corporate ads, street names, maps and post-9/11 security terminology.

The Institute's research performances are often accompanied by websites, workshops, gallery installations, and publications (like this one) that instigate public reflection, dialogue and action.

MORE PROJECTS BY THE INSTITUTE

Corporate Commands
www.corporatecommands.com

The City Formerly Known as Cambridge
www.ikatun.com/institute/rename

57 Things to Do For Free in Harvard Square
www.ikatun.com/57

42 or 363 Definitions of Cartography
www.lulu.com/content/417228

The Analysis of Infinitely Small Things
www.ikatun.com/k/infinitelysmallthings/

CPSIA information can be obtained at www.ICGtesting.com
Printed in the USA
LVOW081858040912

297331LV00002B/218/A

9 781430 319863